Dare to Dream

Children's Leader Guide

Dare to Dream
Series

Dare to Dream:
Creating a God-Sized Mission Statement for Your Life
978-1-4267-7577-2

Dare to Dream
DVD
978-1-4267-7578-9

Dare to Dream
Leader Guide
978-1-4267-7579-6

Dare to Dream
Youth Book
978-1-4267-7580-2

Dare to Dream
Youth DVD
978-1-4267-7582-6

Dare to Dream
Children's Leader Guide
978-1-4267-7581-9

Dare to Dream
Preview Book
978-1-4267-7583-3

Mike Slaughter

Dare to Dream

Creating a God-Sized
Mission Statement for Your Life

Children's Leader Guide

by Sally Hoelscher

Abingdon Press
Nashville

Mike Slaughter

Dare to Dream:
Creating a God-Sized Mission Statement for Your Life

Children's Leader Guide
by Sally Hoelscher

Library of Congress Cataloging-in-Publication applied for.

ISBN 978-1-4267-7581-9

13 14 15 16 17 18 19 20 21 22—10 9 8 7 6 5 4 3 2 1

MANUFACTURED IN THE UNITED STATES OF AMERICA

CONTENTS

To the Leader 6

1. God's Presence 8

2. God's Plans 18

3. Messages from God 28

4. No Excuses 38

5. Use Your Gifts 46

6. Keep Loving God 54

To the Leader

Dare to Dream is a series that encourages people to explore God's dream for them, create a life mission statement, and put it to work in their daily lives. Because the series includes studies for adults, youth, and children, it can be effectively used as an all-church study. This Children's Leader Guide contains session ideas for younger children (5–7) and older children (8–11), including reproducible handouts.

The lessons in this guide are presented in a large group/small group format. Children begin with time spent at activity centers followed by time together as a large group. Children end the lesson in small groups determined by age. Each lesson plan contains the following sections.

Focus for the Teacher

The information in this section will provide you with background information about the Bible story and Bible verse for the week. Use this section for your own study as you prepare the week's lesson.

Explore Interest Groups

Ideas for a variety of activity centers will be found in this section. These activities will prepare the children to hear the Bible story. Allow the children to choose one or more of the activities that interest them.

Large Group

The children will come together as a large group to hear the Bible story. This section also contains an activity related to the Bible verse.

Small Groups

Children are divided into age-level groups for small-group time. Depending on the size of your class, you may need to have more than one group for each age level. It is recommended that each small group contain no more than ten children.

Younger Children
The activities in this section are designed for children five to seven years old.

Older Children
The activities in this section are designed for children eight to eleven years old.

Reproducible Pages

At the end of each lesson are reproducible pages, to be photocopied and handed out for all the children to use during that lesson's activities.

Schedule

Many churches have weeknight programs that include an evening meal, an intergenerational gathering time, and classes for children, youth, and adults. The following schedule illustrates one way to organize a weeknight program.

5:30	Meal
6:00	Intergenerational gathering
6:15–8:15	Classes for children, youth, and adults

Churches may want to do this study as a Sunday school program. This setting would be similar to the weeknight setting. The following schedule takes into account a shorter class time that is the norm for Sunday morning programs.

10 minutes	Intergenerational gathering
45 minutes	Classes for children, youth, and adults

Choose a schedule that works best for your congregation and its Christian education programs.

Blessings to you and the children as you dare to dream!

1 God's Presence

Objectives
The children will
- hear Genesis 28:10-22.
- learn how God spoke to Jacob through a dream.
- discover that God is always with them.
- explore what it means to live in God's presence.

Bible Story
Jacob's Dream
(Genesis 28:10-22)

Bible Verse
Lord, you have examined me.
You know me. (Psalm 139:1)

Focus for the Teacher

Jacob's Dream

As we encounter Jacob in today's Bible story, he is on the run. Having tricked his father, Isaac, into giving him the blessing meant for his older brother, Esau, it is no longer safe for Jacob to remain at home. In order to escape Esau's plan to kill him, Jacob leaves to go live with his mother's family. Along the way Jacob stops for the night. While he is asleep, God appears to Jacob in his dream. God's message to Jacob is a promise of land, many descendants, and protection. Jacob is also promised God's presence, now and always.

> God will always be with us.

The Bible Verse

In each of the six sessions in this study, the Bible verse for the lesson is one verse from Psalm 139, beginning with verse one and proceeding through the sixth verse. The keyword in Psalm 139 is *know*. In the first six verses of this psalm the word *know* appears three times, and a form of the word (*knowledge*) is used an additional time. Throughout the study, these verses will help us explore what it means to be known by God.

God's Presence

When Jacob awakens from his dream, he realizes its significance. Being on the run as he is, Jacob is likely afraid and uncertain of his future. God's promise to be with him, now and always, changes everything. During the course of this study, the children in your class will be encouraged to consider God's plans for their lives. As children, they are still in the process of discovering their gifts and talents and the ways they are called to live into God's dreams for them. Regardless of what they are called to be now and in the future, one thing is certain: God is with each one of them, just as God was with Jacob—now and always.

Explore Interest Groups

Be sure that adult leaders are waiting when the first child arrives. Greet and welcome the children. Get the children involved in an activity that interests them and introduces the theme for the day's activities.

Black-and-White Dreams

- **Say:** Usually when we think about drawing a black-and-white picture, we are referring to black writing on a white piece of paper. Today you will use white crayon to draw on black paper.

- Invite each child to think about dreams he or she may have had.

- Encourage the children to draw a picture about a dream that they remember.

- **Say:** Our Bible story today is about a dream.

Prepare

✓ Provide black construction paper and white crayons.

✓ **Note:** If the children cannot remember a dream, encourage them to draw a picture about a dream they would like to have.

Stuck Together

- **Ask:** Can you link these two paper clips together without touching them?

- Give each child a strip of paper.

- Have each child form the paper into a loose *S*-shape.

- Have each child use one paper clip to attach the top of the *S* to the center of the *S* about ½ to 1 inch from the end of the strip.

- Have each child use the other paper clip to attach the bottom of the *S* to the center of the *S* about ½ to 1 inch from the other end of the strip.

- Have each child hold one end of the paper strip in each hand and pull quickly to straighten out the paper strip.

- **Ask:** What happened to the paper clips?

- **Say:** These paper clips are now stuck together. Today we are going to be talking about God being stuck on us!

- Have the children experiment with trying to make a longer paper clip chain using this method.

Prepare

✓ Provide paper cut into 11-inch by 1½-inch strips and paper clips.

✓ Give each child two paper clips.

Prepare

✓ Use masking tape to designate a starting line and a finish line on opposite sides of the room.

Staircase Relay

- Divide the children into teams with an even number of players on each team.

- Have each child partner with another child on that team.

- Have the teams line up at the starting line with partners standing together.

- Instruct the children to sit down with their legs extending in front of them. Partners should be facing each other with their feet touching.

- **Say:** Your team has now formed a staircase. The children closest to the starting line form the top step. The children farthest from the starting line form the bottom step. Your job is to move your staircase across the room to the finish line. Here is how you will do that. When I say go, those of you who are forming the bottom step will jump up and run to the top of the staircase. You will sit back down right next to those forming the top step and when your feet are again touching you will say, "Move up!" When you say "Move up!" the new bottom step may move to the top. Continue moving in this way until the top rung of your ladder is on the finish line.

- Encourage children to play the game. If time permits, have the children move their staircases back to the starting line.

- **Say:** In our Bible story today, we will hear about someone who has a dream about a staircase.

Large Group

Bring all the children together to experience the Bible story. Use a bell to alert the children to the large-group time.

Jacob's Dream

- **Say:** Our Bible story today is found in the book of Genesis.

- **Ask:** Where do we find Genesis in the Bible? (In the Old Testament. Genesis is the first book of the Bible.)

- Show the family tree you have drawn.

- **Say:** You have probably heard stories about Abraham. Abraham and Sarah had a son when they were both very old. Their son's name was Isaac. Isaac married Rebekah, and they had twin sons named Jacob and Esau. Our story today is about Jacob.

- **Ask:** What was the relationship between Jacob and Abraham? (Abraham was Jacob's grandfather.)

- Read the Bible story from the "Jacob's Dream" handout, pausing to ask the children the questions in italicized print. Be affirming of the children's answers. There are no right or wrong answers to these questions.

- **Say:** God promised always to be with Jacob. God makes that same promise to us. God is always with us, no matter where we are or what we are doing. God is with us!

- **Ask:** How does it make you feel to know God is always with you?

Prepare

✓ Photocopy the "Jacob's Dream" handout at the end of this lesson for each child to take home.

✓ On a marker board or a piece of mural paper, draw a family tree for Jacob and place it where it can easily be seen. At the top of the tree, place Abraham and Sarah. Draw a line down from Abraham and Sarah to connect to their son, Isaac. Write Rebekah next to Isaac's name. Draw two lines down from Isaac and Rebekah to connect to their sons, Esau and Jacob.

God Knows You

- **Say:** Not only do we know that God is always with us, but God also knows all about us. Our Bible verse for today is the first verse of Psalm 139.

- Invite the children to read the Bible verse with you as you read it aloud.

- **Say:** Now let's put some actions to our Bible verse.

Prepare

✓ Write the Bible verse on a marker board or a piece of mural paper and place it where it can be easily seen. (LORD, you have examined me. You know me. —Psalm 139:1)

- Teach the children the following actions:

  o Lord, (Point up.)
  o you have examined me. (Make circles with both hands and hold them up to your eyes as if you are looking through binoculars. Look all over the room.)
  o You (Point up again.)
  o know me. (Point to yourself.)

- Encourage the children to say the Bible verse with you several times while doing the actions.

God Is With Us

- **Ask:** In Jacob's dream, where did God promise to be? (With Jacob) For how long? (Always)

- **Say:** God promises to be with us, too. Always! We are going to say a litany right now to remind us that God is with us.

- Ask the children with pieces of paper to stand up.

- **Say:** The people who are standing are going to take turns saying, "When we are…" and then reading what is on the piece of paper I have given them. After each person reads, our response will be, "God is with us!"

- Have the class practice their response.

- Have the children who are standing take turns saying, "When we are…" and reading their pieces of paper. Encourage the class to respond after each reading with the words "God is with us!"

- Finish the litany by saying, "No matter where we are, who we are with, or what we are feeling…" and encourage the class to respond, "God is with us!"

- Dismiss children to their small groups.

Prepare

✓ On separate, small pieces of paper, write the following words: "at home," "at school," "on vacation," "on the playground," "at the mall," "at church," "with friends," "with family," "alone," "feeling happy," "feeling sad," "discouraged," "scared."

✓ Give each piece of paper to a child in your class who is comfortable reading aloud.

Small Groups

Divide the children into small groups. You may organize the groups around age levels or around readers and nonreaders. Keep the groups small, with a maximum of ten children in each group. You may need to have more than one group of each age level.

Younger Children (Ages 5-7)

- **Ask:** In our Bible story today, how did Jacob know God was with him? (God told him in a dream.)

- **Say:** Many of us have not had Jacob's experience of hearing God speak to us. Yet we know God is with each one of us.

- **Ask:** How do you know God is with you? Are there certain places where you feel closer to God? Are there people who help you feel God's presence?

- Allow children time to share. Assure children that there are no right or wrong answers. Each of us experiences God's presence in our own way.

- Give each child a piece of paper.

- **Say:** In Jacob's dream he saw a staircase going from earth up to heaven. Some translations of the Bible use the word *ladder* instead of staircase. You may have heard the expression, "Jacob's Ladder."

- Encourage the children to use the craft sticks to make a ladder or staircase on their paper, gluing the sticks to the paper. The craft stick may be cut or broken into smaller pieces.

- Have the children use the markers to write on their ladders the words "God is always with me."

- Encourage the children to use crayons and markers to decorate their pictures.

- **Say:** Your picture can help remind you of Jacob's dream and of God's presence with you always.

- **Pray:** Loving God, thank you for being with us. Help us to feel your presence and remember we are never alone. Amen.

Prepare

✓ Provide paper, crayons, craft sticks, scissors, markers, and glue.

Prepare

✓ Photocopy the "Dreams in the Bible" handout at the end of this lesson for each child.

✓ Provide Bibles, paper, pencils, colored pencils, scissors, tape, and chenille stems.

Older Children (Ages 8–11)

- **Ask:** In our Bible story today, how did Jacob know God was with him? (God told him in a dream.)

- **Say:** Jacob is not the only person who received a message from God in a dream.

- Give each child a copy of the "Dreams in the Bible" handout and a pencil.

- Together as a group, look up the Bible stories and complete the worksheet.

- **Ask:** Have you ever heard God talking to you in a dream?

- **Say:** Many of us have not had Jacob's experience of hearing God speak to us. Yet we know God is with each one of us.

- **Ask:** How do you know God is with you? Are there certain places where you feel closer to God? Are there people who help you feel God's presence? Have there been times when you felt far from God?

- Allow children time to share. Assure children that there are no right or wrong answers. Each of us experiences God's presence in our own way.

- **Say:** In Jacob's dream he saw a staircase going from earth up to heaven. Some translations of the Bible use the word *ladder* instead of staircase. You may have heard the expression "Jacob's Ladder."

- Encourage each child to use the chenille stems to make a ladder or a staircase.

- Have each child cut a small pennant or banner shape from a piece of paper and write on it the words "God is always with me."

- Have the children tape their banner to the ladder or staircase.

- **Say:** When you take your ladders and staircases home, they can help you remember Jacob's dream and God's promise to be with you always.

- **Pray:** God, thank you for loving us. Thank you for your promise to be with us always. Help us to remember your promise and to be aware of your presence. Amen.

Jacob's Dream

Based on Genesis 28:10-22

Jacob's brother, Esau, was mad at him. Esau was so furious that Jacob feared for his life. Jacob and Esau's mother decided it would be a good idea for Jacob to go away for a while until Esau calmed down. So Jacob left home.

How do you think Jacob was feeling?

Jacob had a long journey ahead of him. He was going to stay with his mother's family where he would be safe. After traveling all day, Jacob stopped to rest. When the sun went down, Jacob got ready to go to sleep. He found a big stone and used it for a pillow.

Have you ever used a rock for a pillow? How would it feel?

Jacob dreamed that there was a big staircase extending from earth up to the sky. God's messengers were going up and down the staircase. Suddenly God was in Jacob's dream, standing at the top of the ladder.

Have you ever dreamed about God or heaven or angels?

In Jacob's dream, God said, "I am the God of your grandfather, Abraham, and the God of your father, Isaac. I am with you now. I will protect you everywhere you go and I will bring you back to this land. I will give you and your descendants the land you are lying on. I will never leave you."

How do you think Jacob felt when he woke up?

When Jacob woke up, he thought to himself, "I didn't realize it, but now I know that God is here!" Jacob took the stone that he had slept on, set it upright, and poured oil on the top of it. Jacob did these things to mark the place as special. Jacob named the place "Bethel," which means God's house.

Why do you think Jacob chose the name God's house? Is God only found at the place where Jacob slept?

Jacob said, "God has promised to be with me and protect me on this trip. I have set this stone as a sacred pillar and a reminder of God's message to me on this spot."

How do you think it made Jacob feel to know that God would always be with him? How did Jacob's feelings change through this story?

Dreams in the Bible

The Bible contains many stories of God sending messages through dreams. Use your Bible to look up each story listed below in the right column. Draw a line connecting each story to the person in the left column who received a message from God in a dream.

Pharaoh	Matthew 1:18-24
Jacob	1 Kings 3:5-14
Joseph	Genesis 28:10-17
Solomon	Matthew 2:1-12
Magi (wise men)	Genesis 41:1-7, 15-16, 25-30

2 God's Plans

<table>
<tr><td>

Objectives

The children will
- hear Jeremiah 29:11-14a.
- learn how Jeremiah told people about God's plans for them.
- discover that God has a plan for them.
- explore what it means to search for God's plan for their lives.

</td><td>

Bible Story

Jeremiah's Message
(Jeremiah 29:11-14a)

Bible Verse

You know when I sit down and when I stand up. Even from far away, you comprehend my plans. (Psalm 139:2)

</td></tr>
</table>

Focus for the Teacher

Jeremiah's Message

Jeremiah knew firsthand that it was not easy to be God's prophet. Jeremiah had the unenviable task of delivering messages from God that God's people did not want to hear. Jeremiah warned the Israelites that their homeland was going to be invaded and that those who survived were going to be sent into exile. Not all of Jeremiah's messages contained bad news. When the Israelites were in exile in Babylon, Jeremiah delivered a message of hope. Jeremiah assured God's people that God was still with them and encouraged them to look to the future with hope.

> God has plans for each one of us.

The Bible Verse

Not only does God have a plan in mind for us, but God knows our plans. As we continue looking at Psalm 139, we are reminded that God knows our every action and all of our thoughts. The psalmist, who might have been King David, affirms that our lives come from God; God does not desert us but rather knows everything we do.

God's Plans

Jeremiah's message to the Israelites still speaks to us today. "I know the plans I have in mind for you, declares the LORD; they are plans for peace, not disaster, to give you a future filled with hope" (Jeremiah 29:11). It may be tempting to read this verse and decide that God plans every single thing we do. But to do so denies that God created human beings with choices. Yes, God has a plan in mind for us, but that plan is affected by what we do. We are faced with many choices. We may even choose whether or not to try and discern God's plan for us. And God says, "When you search for me, yes, search for me with all your heart, you will find me." (Jeremiah 29:13)

Explore Interest Groups

Be sure that adult leaders are waiting when the first child arrives. Greet and welcome the children. Get the children involved in an activity that interests them and introduces the theme for the day's activities.

The Searching Game

- Have the children form a circle on the outside of the string.

- Choose one child to stand in the middle of the circle.

- Have the children reach down and pick up the string, holding it in both of their hands, and taking a step backward or forward as needed so the circle of string is taut.

- **Say:** You will notice there is one bead on our string circle. We are going to pass the bead around the circle trying to keep it hidden so the person in the middle cannot tell where it is. Let's practice.

- Have the children practice hiding the bead in their hands and moving their hands along the circle to pass the bead on to the next person. Encourage the children to keep moving their hands even when they don't have the bead.

- **Say:** I am going to start the music. While the music is playing, keep passing the bead. When the music stops, the person who has the bead should hang on to it.

- Start the music and encourage the children to pass the bead.

- Stop the music and have the child in the middle guess which child is holding the bead. If the guess is correct, have the children change places. You might wish to give younger children more than one guess.

- **Say:** You have been searching for the bead. When we hear our Bible story today, we will be talking about searching for God.

Prepare

✓ Provide CD of Christian music, CD player, bead, string, and scissors.

✓ Set up the CD player to play the music you have selected.

✓ Cut a piece of string approximately 20 feet long.

✓ Thread the bead onto the string and tie the ends of the string together, forming a circle of string.

✓ Lay the circle of string on the floor in an open area.

✓ **Note:** If you have a large class, prepare more than one beaded string and divide the class into groups, having all the groups use the same musical cues.

Prepare

✓ Photocopy the "What's the Design?" handout at the end of this lesson. You will need at least two copies per child.

✓ Provide crayons.

Discover the Design

- Divide the children into two equal groups. Have each group sit at a separate table or in a separate area so that they may not observe each other's work.

- Give each child a copy of the "What's the Design?" handout.

- Invite the children to color in the grid using the colors and designs of their choice.

- When all children are finished making a design, have one group of children turn their designs facedown on the table to be used later. Give each child in this group another copy of the "What's the Design?" handout.

- Invite the other group of children to bring their designs over to where the first group was working. Have each child in the second group stand or sit back-to-back with one of the children in the first group.

- **Say:** Some of you have a blank grid in front of you. The person behind you has a decorated grid. Your challenge is to copy their design without looking at it. You may ask any question that can be answered in one word, such as, "Is every square in your design colored in?" or "Is the first square in the first row red?" Those of you who have designs in front of you may answer the questions asked, but you may not provide additional information.

- Encourage the children to complete the task.

- After a certain time, have the children compare their designs.

- **Ask:** What made that task easy or difficult? How did you feel when you were trying to figure out the design? Did you ever feel like giving up?

- Have the children switch places and repeat the challenge.

- **Say:** You have been trying to figure out what your friends want you to do. Today in our Bible story, we are going to talk about figuring out what God wants us to do.

Large Group

Bring all the children together to experience the Bible story. Use a bell to alert the children to the large-group time.

Jeremiah's Message

- **Say:** Our Bible story today is about a prophet named Jeremiah. A prophet is someone who delivers messages from God. Sometimes people get mad at prophets because they don't want to hear God's message. Other times prophets speak reassuring messages reminding people of God's love for them. Let's hear Jeremiah's message.

- Read the Bible story from the "Jeremiah's Message" handout.

- **Say:** God's people had messed up. They had been ignoring God and not following God's rules. When Jeremiah warned them there would be consequences for their actions, they ignored Jeremiah, too.

- **Ask:** What was God's message that was sent through Jeremiah? (God has a plan for God's people. It is a good plan.) What did Jeremiah tell the people to do in order to discover God's plan? (Search for God with all their heart.)

- **Say:** Jeremiah told the people that God had a good plan for them. Jeremiah also reassured the people that God hadn't forgotten them and was still with them. One way we search for God and connect with God is through prayer. Jeremiah also reminded the people to pray.

God Knows Your Plans

- **Say:** Not only does God have a plan for us, but God also knows all our plans. Our Bible verse for today is the second verse of Psalm 139.

- Invite the children to read the Bible verse with you.

- **Say:** Now let's put some actions to our Bible verse.

- Have the children stand up. Teach them the following actions:

  o You know when I sit down (Sit down.)
  o and when I stand up. (Stand up.)
  o Even from far away, (Put hand above eyes and pretend you are looking for something far away.)
  o you completely comprehend my plans. (Put your index finger on your temple and nod.)

Prepare

✓ Photocopy the handout "Jeremiah's Message" at the end of this lesson for each child to take home.

Prepare

✓ Write the Bible verses for last week and this week on a marker board or a piece of mural paper and place it where it can be easily seen. (LORD, you have examined me. You know me. You know when I sit down and when I stand up. Even from far away, you comprehend my plans. —Psalm 139:1-2)

✓ Cover last week's verse with a piece of paper so that only the verse for this week is visible.

✓ Review the actions that went with last week's verse.

- Encourage the children to say the Bible verse with you while doing the actions.

- Uncover last week's Bible verse.

- **Say:** Now let's add this week's verse to last week's verse.

- Review the actions for last week's verse and then encourage the children to say both verses with you while doing both sets of actions.

Active Praying

- **Say:** Jeremiah's message to God's people is for us, too. We are God's people. God has a good plan for us. It is important for us to remember to pray to God and keep trying to figure out what God wants us to do. Often we think about bowing our heads and folding our hands to pray. That's okay, but there are many other prayer positions, too. Let's say some active prayers. I'll give you an action to do, and then I will say a short prayer while you are doing it.

- Lead the children in the following actions and prayers.

  o Stand up and turn slowly around in a circle.
  o **Pray:** God, we are searching for you with our whole heart.
  o Jog in place.
  o **Pray:** God, use our feet to take us places you want us to go.
  o Stand still and stretch your hands out to the sides. Wiggle your fingers.
  o **Pray:** God, use our hands to do your work in the world.
  o Take a deep breath in and then let it out.
  o **Pray:** God, thank you for always loving us and always being with us. Amen.

- Dismiss the children to their small groups.

Small Groups

Divide the children into small groups. You may organize the groups around age levels or around readers and nonreaders. Keep the groups small, with a maximum of ten children in each group. You may need to have more than one group of each age level.

Younger Children (Ages 5–7)

- **Ask:** What is a plan? When do you make a plan?

- **Say:** Jeremiah tells us that God has a plan in mind for our lives. Not only that, but it is a good plan!

- **Ask:** How does it make you feel to know God has plans for you?

- **Say:** This doesn't mean that every single thing you do is planned out for you. God gave human beings the ability to make choices. You get to choose what you do. You even get to choose whether or not to follow God's plan. But God wants what is best for each one of us. You already know many of the things God wants you to do.

- **Ask:** What are some things God wants you to do? (Possible answers may include but are not limited to: Follow Jesus' teachings. Love one another. Be kind. Help each other.)

- **Say:** As you continue to grow and you continue to pray, you will discover more of God's plan for your life.

- Give each child a copy of the prayer you have made.

- **Say:** Jeremiah encourages us to pray to God to know what God wants us to do. Here is a simple prayer that you can take home and pray every day.

- Read the prayer that you wrote on the prayer sheet inside the large heart.

- Hand out the prayer sheets, and encourage the children to decorate their sheets.

- **Pray:** God, help each one of us know what you want us to do. Amen.

Prepare

✓ Draw a large heart on a piece of paper. Inside the heart, write the words "God, help me know what you want me to do. Amen." Photocopy this page for each child.

✓ Provide crayons.

Prepare

✓ Provide paper and colored pencils.

Older Children (Ages 8–11)

- **Say:** Jeremiah tells us that God has a plan in mind for our lives. Not only that, but it is a good plan!

- **Ask:** How does it make you feel to know God has plans for you? Do you know what God's plan is for you?

- **Say:** This doesn't mean that every single thing you do is planned out for you. God gave human beings the ability to make choices. You get to choose what you do. You even get to choose whether or not to follow God's plan. But God wants what is best for each one of us.

- **Ask:** Do you know some of God's plans for you? What are some things God wants you to do? (Possible answers may include but are not limited to: Follow Jesus' teachings. Love one another. Be kind. Help each other.)

- **Say:** As you continue to grow and continue to pray, you will discover more of God's plan for your life. You can pray for God to help you know what God wants you to do.

- Give each child a piece of paper.

- Encourage the children to write a one-sentence prayer asking for God to help them know what to do.

- Offer encouragement and examples if needed. Some examples are: Loving God, guide me on your path. God, help me know what to do. Holy One, show me your way.

- **Say:** This is a good prayer to say every day or any time when you are not sure what to do.

- **Pray:** God, thank you for your constant presence in our lives. Help us understand how you want us to live and then give us the courage to do your work. Amen.

What's the Design?

Jeremiah's Message

Based on Jeremiah 29:11-14*a*

God's people were sad. The place where they had been living had been invaded. Many people died, and those who survived were sent away to live in a strange place.

The prophet Jeremiah had warned God's people that this would happen if they continued to disobey God. Now Jeremiah could have said, "I told you so!" But instead, God had Jeremiah deliver a message of hope.

Jeremiah told the people, "This is what God says: 'I know the plans I have in mind for you; they are plans for peace, not disaster. I will give you a future filled with hope. When you call me and pray to me, I will listen to you. When you search for me, yes, search for me with all your heart, you will find me. I will be present for you.'"

3 Messages from God

Objectives
The children will:
- hear Exodus 3:1-10.
- learn that God spoke to Moses from a burning bush.
- discover that God still speaks to us today.
- explore what it means to listen for God's messages.

Bible Story
Moses and the Burning Bush
(Exodus 3:1-10)

Bible Verse
You study my traveling and resting.
    You are thoroughly familiar with all my ways. (Psalm 139:3)

Focus for the Teacher

Moses and the Burning Bush

God called Moses in a very dramatic way, by speaking from a burning bush. Moses could have walked by the burning bush and missed God's call, but instead he was paying attention and chose to investigate. In order to hear God's call in our own lives, we need to pay attention. God called Moses by name. This was not a burning bush meant for anyone who happened to walk by; God had a plan specifically for Moses.

The Bible Verse

We continue our progress through Psalm 139 by looking at verse 3 this week. This verse repeats the idea that God knows us through and through. God knows everything about us. This is a thought that can be reassuring and overwhelming at the same time.

God is still speaking.

Messages from God

Most of us have never experienced God speaking to us from a burning bush. That doesn't mean that God doesn't have a plan for us. God's message for us today tends to be delivered in more subtle ways. Help your children understand that God still communicates with us today, though in a different way than God spoke to Moses. God has called you to teach children. You are making a difference in God's world in the lives of children. Through teaching and caring for the children in your class, you can help them hear the messages God has for them.

Explore Interest Groups

Be sure that adult leaders are waiting when the first child arrives. Greet and welcome the children. Get the children involved in an activity that interests them and introduces the theme for the day's activities.

What's the Message?

- Show the children the pieces of paper you have prepared.

- **Say:** These pages contain messages for you that are waiting to be discovered.

- Have each child choose a piece of paper.

- Show the children how to use the side of the marker tip to color back and forth over the paper to make the writing appear.

God Has a Message For...

- Choose one child to stand in the center of the circle of chairs. Have the rest of the children sit in the chairs.

- Explain the following rules to the children:

  o The person in the center will say, "God has a message for…" and complete the statement by saying something that is true about him or her. For example: "God has a message for people wearing socks," "God has a message for anyone who plays the flute," or "God has a message for people whose favorite color is green."

  o Every person in the circle for whom that statement is true must get up and find a new seat at least two chairs away from where they were sitting, while the person in the middle tries to get a seat also.

  o The person left standing becomes the next person to deliver a message.

- Encourage the children to play the game.

Prepare

✓ Use a white crayon to write messages on white pieces of paper. Use the sample messages shown or make up your own. You will need a message for each child.

✓ Sample messages: God loves you. God will always be with you. God has a good plan for you. Pray every day. God knows your name.

✓ Provide markers.

Prepare

✓ Form a circle of chairs facing inward, using one less chair than the number of children playing the game.

Prepare

✓ Provide pretzel sticks, grated cheddar cheese, plates, and napkins.

A Fiery Snack

- Have the children wash their hands.

- **Say:** In our Bible story today, we are going to hear about something that was on fire. Right now we are going to make a fire we can eat.

- Give each child a paper plate and a handful of pretzel sticks.

- Encourage the children to place their pretzel sticks in a pile so they look like a pile of sticks.

- Sprinkle grated cheese on top of each child's pretzel pile so it resembles a fire.

- Say a prayer of thanks and enjoy the snack together.

Large Group

Bring all the children together to experience the Bible story. Use a bell to alert the children to the large-group time.

Moses and the Burning Bush

- **Say:** Today we have a visitor who is going to share his story with us.

- Introduce Moses and let him tell his story from Moses and the Burning Bush.

- Encourage the children to be good listeners. Compliment them for being polite.

- Thank Moses for sharing his story.

- **Ask:** How do you think Moses felt when he realized God was speaking to him out of the burning bush? Why do you think God chose a burning bush to speak to Moses? What would your response be if a burning bush called out your name?

- **Say:** God had a job that needed to be done; the Israelites needed to be freed from slavery in Egypt. God chose Moses for that job.

God Knows All of Your Ways

- **Say:** The message God spoke from the burning bush wasn't for just anyone who wandered by. God called Moses by name. God knew Moses, and God knows us. Our Bible verse for today is the third verse of Psalm 139.

- Invite the children to read the Bible verse with you.

- **Say:** Now let's put some actions to our Bible verse.

- Have the children stand up.

- Teach the children the following actions:

  o You study my traveling (Walk in place.)
  o and resting. (Stand still.)
  o You are thoroughly familiar with all my ways. (Point in many different directions. Keep pointing in different directions until the verse is finished.)

Prepare

✓ Photocopy the "Moses and the Burning Bush" handout at the end of this lesson for each child to take home.

✓ Recruit a volunteer (boy or girl) who is willing to come in and tell the story as Moses. The reader may wear a shepherd's costume if one is available.

Prepare

✓ Write the Bible verses for the last two weeks and this week on a marker board or a piece of mural paper and place it where it can be easily seen. (LORD, you have examined me. You know me. You know when I sit down and when I stand up. Even from far away, you comprehend my plans. You study my traveling and resting. You are thoroughly familiar with all my ways. —Psalm 139:1-3)

✓ Cover verses 1-2 with a piece of paper so that only the verse for this week is visible.

✓ Review the actions for the previous verses.

- Encourage the children to say the Bible verse with you while doing the actions.

- Uncover the previous verses.

- **Say:** Now let's add this week's verse to our previous verses.

- Review the actions for the verses and then encourage the children to say all the verses with you while doing the actions.

Prepare

✓ Look through some magazines for interesting pictures of our world. Find nature photos and photos with people in them. For example you might use: a waterfall, children playing together, a person who is ill, mountains, people who appear hungry or in need of other assistance, people of different cultures interacting together, a sunset, people sharing a meal together, and so forth.

✓ Cut the pictures out and mount each one on a piece of construction paper.

✓ Optional: If you have access to a computer and projector, you may prepare a slide show of images to show.

Messages from God

- **Say:** Although most of us will never hear God speaking to us from a burning bush as Moses did, we can still hear God speaking to us. God may not speak to us in a voice that we can hear, as God spoke to Moses, but we can hear God speaking to us through the world around us. We are going to look at some pictures and think about what message God might have for us.

- One at a time, show the children the pictures you have prepared ahead of time.

- **Ask:** What might God be saying in this picture?

- Allow time for the children to respond, keeping in mind that there are no wrong answers. God can say more than one thing through the same image.

- If the children appear stuck for ideas, ask questions to help them get started. Does this picture remind you of any Bible stories you know? What do you feel when you look at this picture?

- **Say:** If Moses had not been paying attention, he might have missed God calling to him from the burning bush. We also need to pay attention if we are to hear the messages God has for us.

- Dismiss children to their small groups.

Small Groups

Divide the children into small groups. You may organize the groups around age levels or around readers and nonreaders. Keep the groups small, with a maximum of ten children in each group. You may need to have more than one group of each age level.

Younger Children (Ages 5-7)

- **Say:** Just as God chose Moses to do God's work, God also has a plan for each of us to do God's work. We are called and chosen by God to share God's love with others. By doing so, we can make the world a better place.

- **Ask:** What are some things that God might be calling us to do?

- Affirm the children's answers.

- **Say:** To know what God wants us to do, we need to pay attention, just as Moses was paying attention and noticed the burning bush. We are going to spend some time now being quiet and listening. As you listen, think of one thing that you think God is calling you to do this week.

- Allow time for listening and reflection.

- Give each child a piece of paper.

- Encourage the children to draw a picture showing how they will do God's work this week.

- **Pray:** God, thank you for loving us and choosing us to do your work. Help us to share your love with other people. Amen.

Prepare

✓ Provide paper and crayons.

Prepare

✓ Photocopy the "God's Messages for Us" handout at the end of this lesson for each child. **Answers:** prayer, other people, Bible, nature, worship, silence, dreams.

✓ Provide pencils.

Older Children (Ages 8–11)

- **Say:** Just as God chose Moses to do God's work, God has a plan for us and chooses us to do God's work. Even though God doesn't speak to us from a burning bush, there are other ways that we can discover what God wants us to do.

- Give each child a copy of the "God's Messages for Us" handout and a pencil.

- Encourage the children to unscramble the words and to reflect on what God wants them to do.

- As a group, go over the answers to the scrambled words. For each word, discuss how God might deliver a message through that thing.

- **Say:** It's okay if you are not sure what God's plan for you is. Most people spend their entire lives figuring out what God wants them to do. And God's plan for you will change over time as you grow up. The important thing is to pay attention and to keep praying that God will show you the work God has for you to do.

- **Pray:** God, thank you for your continued presence with us. Thank you for your love that is so great that you know each one of us by name. Please help us know what you want us to do. Amen.

Dare to Dream: Children's Leader Guide

Moses and the Burning Bush

Based on Exodus 3:1-10

Hello! My name is Moses. You may have heard of me. I have many stories I could share with you. Today I'm going to tell you about the time God asked me to help the Israelites.

One day I was taking care of my father-in-law's sheep on Mount Horeb. While I was on the mountain, I saw a bush that was on fire. It was the strangest thing—even though the bush was on fire, it wasn't burning up! I was curious and decided to investigate.

As I came close to the bush, I heard my name: "Moses, Moses!" You can imagine my surprise at hearing a burning bush call my name! Then the voice from the bush told me to take off my shoes because I was standing on holy ground. The voice went on to tell me that it was God talking to me—the God of my father, the God of Abraham and Isaac and Jacob. I was so afraid by this time that I hid my face.

From the burning bush God told me that the Israelites were still slaves in Egypt, and God had heard their cries of suffering. God wanted me to go to Pharaoh (the ruler of Egypt) and bring the Israelites out of Egypt.

I couldn't believe my ears! "Who am I that I should go to Pharaoh and lead your people out of Egypt?" I asked.

And God said, "I will go with you."

I still wasn't sure that I was the right person for the job, but I felt better knowing that I wouldn't be alone. God chose me to lead the Israelites out of Egypt, and God promised to be with me.

What happened next? That's a story for another day.

God's Messages for Us

Although we probably won't experience God speaking from a burning bush, God does choose us to do God's work in the world. Unscramble the words below to discover some places and ways that we might hear and understand God's message for our lives.

YPARER   _____

OHETR LOEEPP   _____

IEBBL   _____

AETURN   _____

SPROIHW   _____

ECNLISE   _____

SDAEMR   _____

Can you think of other ways you might discover what God wants you to do? What do you think God is calling you to do at this time in your life?

4 No Excuses

Objectives
The children will:
- hear Exodus 3:11–4:17.
- learn how Moses tried to get out of rescuing the Israelites.
- discover that when God calls you to do a job God wants you to say yes.
- explore what it means to say yes to God's plan.

Bible Story
Moses Makes Excuses
(Exodus 3:11–4:17)

Bible Verse
There isn't a word on my tongue, LORD,
   that you don't already know completely.
   (Psalm 139:4)

Focus for the Teacher

Moses Makes Excuses
During the last lesson we heard the story of Moses being called by God. You might think that since God called Moses by name and spoke to him from a burning bush, Moses would be willing to do whatever God asked him to do. Not so. Moses tried everything he could think of to change God's mind about choosing him to free the Israelites from slavery. Moses was surprised that God was choosing him. "Who am I to go to Pharaoh and to bring the Israelites out of Egypt?" he asked God in Exodus 3:11. After all, Moses had fled Egypt because he had killed an Egyptian. Yet God chose him to do an important job. To reassure Moses, God gave the same promise given to Jacob and through Jeremiah to God's people: "I'll be with you."

> God does not want excuses.

The Bible Verse
The fourth verse of Psalm 139 reminds us that God not only knows our actions and our plans, but also every word we have ever spoken. Every excuse we have ever tried to use, or might consider using in the future—God knows them all.

No Excuses
Even after God promised to be with him, Moses wasn't finished making excuses: "What am I supposed to say when the Israelites ask who sent me? What if they don't believe me? You know I've never been able to speak well. Please, God, just send someone else." Is it any wonder that the Bible tells us God became angry with Moses? Like Moses, we may be tempted to try to avoid God's plan for our lives. Fortunately, God is persistent and will not give up on us. God will be with us.

Explore Interest Groups

Be sure that adult leaders are waiting when the first child arrives. Greet and welcome the children. Get the children involved in an activity that interests them and introduces the theme for the day's activities.

Excuses Game

- Have the children sit in a circle.

- **Ask:** What's an excuse? (A reason given for not doing something.) Can you give me an example of an excuse?

- **Say:** We are going to play a game to see how many excuses we can come up with. I am going to ask one of you, "_____, will you help me?" That person will respond, "I would, but…" and name an excuse such as "I have to feed my cat," or "I'm just too tired." We will go around the circle, and I will ask each one of you whether you will help. You will answer, "I would, but…" and name every excuse listed so far, then add your own excuse.

- Encourage the children to play the game.

- **Say:** You are creative excuse makers! It has been fun to pretend to make excuses. In our Bible story today, we will hear what happened when Moses tried to make excuses.

Remember God's Presence

- **Say:** In a dream, God promised to be with Jacob. Through Jeremiah, God promised to be with God's people. In our Bible story today, we will hear God promise to be with Moses. God also promises to be with us! Today you will make a picture to take home as a reminder that God is with you.

- Give each child a copy of the "God Is With Me" page.

- Encourage the children to outline each letter with glue, one at a time, and then cut pieces of yarn to place on the glue.

- When all the letters have been outlined with yarn, encourage the children to glue on yarn pieces to decorate the rest of their picture.

Prepare

✓ Photocopy the "God Is With Me" page at the end of this lesson onto cardstock for each child.

✓ Provide yarn, scissors, and glue.

"You've Been Chosen" Tag

- **Say:** We are going to play tag today. I will choose one person to be "It," and he or she will try to tag someone else. If you are tagged, you will become the next "It." The only other rule is that when you are "It" and you tag someone, you must shout, "You've been chosen!"

- Encourage the children to play the game.

Prepare

✓ Identify a large open area free of obstacles, in which to play the game.

Large Group

Bring all the children together to experience the Bible story. Use a bell to alert the children to the large-group time.

Prepare

✓ Photocopy the "Moses Makes Excuses" handout at the end of this lesson for each child to take home.

✓ Recruit a volunteer to help you tell the Bible story.

Prepare

✓ Write the Bible verses for the last three weeks and this week on a marker board or a piece of mural paper and place it where it can be easily seen. (LORD, you have examined me. You know me. You know when I sit down and when I stand up. Even from far away, you comprehend my plans. You study my traveling and resting. You are thoroughly familiar with all my ways. There isn't a word on my tongue, LORD, that you don't already know completely. —Psalm 139:1-4)

✓ Cover verses 1-3 with a piece of paper so that only the verse for this week is visible.

✓ Review the actions for the previous verses.

Moses Makes Excuses

- **Say:** Last week we heard the story of God speaking to Moses.

- **Ask:** How did God speak to Moses? (From a burning bush) What did God ask Moses to do? (Go tell Pharaoh to free the Israelites from slavery)

- **Say:** God was pretty clear about what Moses was supposed to do. There was only one problem. Moses didn't want to do it. As you hear the Bible story, listen for Moses' excuses.

- Read the Bible story from the "Moses Makes Excuses" handout. Have the volunteer you recruited read the words in italics.

- **Ask:** Why do you think Moses kept making excuses to try and get out of what God wanted him to do? What do you think he might have been feeling? (Nervous, afraid, not good enough)

- **Say:** God didn't give up on Moses even when Moses made excuses. God knew Moses was the one to do the job.

God Knows Your Words

Prepare

- **Say:** God knows all about us. God knows everything we do and every word we say.

- Invite the children to read the Bible verse with you.

- **Say:** Now let's put some actions to our Bible verse.

- Have the children stand up.

- Teach the children the following actions:

    o There isn't a word on my tongue, (Point to your mouth.)
    o Lord, (Point to the sky.)
    o that you don't already know completely. (Use one of your index fingers to draw a complete circle.)

- Encourage the children to say the Bible verse with you while doing the actions.

- Uncover the previous verses.

- **Say:** Now let's add this week's verse to our previous verses.

- Review the actions for the verses and then encourage the children to say all of the verses with you while doing the actions.

I Can Do That!

- **Say:** Sometimes when God wants us to do something, we act like Moses and make excuses. Right now let's practice *not* making excuses. I'm going to ask you some questions. Your response is, "I can do that!"

- Read the following questions, pausing after each to allow children to respond. Encourage the children to respond enthusiastically.

    o Can you be a friend to a new kid at school?
    o Can you cheer up someone who is sad?
    o Can you invite someone to come to church with you?
    o Can you tell people God loves them?
    o Can you help raise money to do God's work?
    o Can you say yes to doing God's work?

- Dismiss children to their small groups.

Small Groups

Divide the children into small groups. You may organize the groups around age levels or around readers and nonreaders. Keep the groups small, with a maximum of ten children in each group. You may need to have more than one group of each age level.

Prepare

✓ On a large piece of poster board, write the words, "We can do God's work!"

✓ Provide markers.

Younger Children (Ages 5–7)

- **Ask:** What did God ask Moses to do? (Go tell Pharaoh to free the Israelites.) What did Moses say? (He made excuses.) Did God give up on Moses? (No.)

- **Say:** When God wants us to do something, we might want to make excuses. Maybe we don't think we can do what God wants us to do. But God will help us. And with God's help, there is no reason for excuses.

- Show children the poster you have made.

- Together as a group, read what the poster says.

- Have each child sign his or her name to the poster.

- Encourage the children to work together to decorate the poster.

- **Ask:** What are some things you can do to share God's love?

- Help the children find a place to hang their poster.

- **Pray:** God, sometimes you ask us to do things we aren't sure we can do. With your help we will make no excuses. We will do your work! Amen.

Older Children (Ages 8–11)

- **Ask:** What did God ask Moses to do? (Go tell Pharaoh to free the Israelites) What did Moses say? (He made excuses) Did God give up on Moses? (No)

- **Say:** Think about a time when you had to do something you didn't want to do.

- **Ask:** Did you make excuses? Were you able to get out of what you were supposed to do?

- **Say:** When God wants us to do something, we might want to make excuses. Maybe we don't think we can do what God wants us to do. Or maybe we are doing something else that seems more exciting. As we heard in the story of Moses, when God wants us to do something, God keeps asking and doesn't accept excuses.

- **Ask:** What promise did God make Moses? (To be with him)

- **Say:** No matter what God wants you to do, God will help you do it. God will be with you. Today we are going to make "No Excuses" posters to hang up around the church.

- Give each child a piece of cardstock.

- **Say:** Make a poster that shows you are willing to do God's work. The poster might say, "I make no excuses to God!" or "I can do God's work!"

- Encourage each child to make and decorate a poster.

- Help the children find places to hang up their posters.

- **Pray:** God, we are ready to do your work. Even when we are unsure about what you want us to do, we will trust you. We will make no excuses! Amen.

Prepare
✓ Provide cardstock and markers.

Moses Makes Excuses

Based on Exodus 3:11–4:17

One day while Moses was taking care of his father-in-law's animals, God spoke to him from a burning bush. God said, "Moses, my people are slaves in Egypt. I am sending you to Pharaoh to bring my people, the Israelites, out of Egypt." Moses, however, had several excellent excuses.

Excuse #1: God, I think you have the wrong guy. Who am I to go to Pharaoh and ask him to free the Israelites?

God said, "Moses, you are the one I have chosen for this job. And I will be with you!

Excuse #2: But, God, if I go to the Israelites and tell them the God of their ancestors sent me to free them, they're going to ask me your name. I don't know what to tell them.

God said, "I Am Who I Am. Tell the Israelites that I Am sent you. Tell them Abraham's God, Isaac's God, and Jacob's God sent you."

Excuse #3: The Israelites might not believe me. What if they say, "God didn't appear to you!"

God said, "I will give you signs to perform that will make them believe. When you throw your staff on the ground, it will become a snake. When you pick up the snake by its tail, it will become your staff again."

Excuse #4: God, I've never been good at speaking. I'm sure I wouldn't know the words to say.

God said, "Who gives people the ability to speak? Isn't it I, the Lord? Now go! I'll help you speak, and I'll teach you what to say.

Excuse #5: Moses had run out of excuses. He said, "Please, God, just send someone else."

God said, "Moses, no more excuses! You are the one I have chosen to do this job. Your brother, Aaron, is a good speaker. Take him with you, and he will help you. But you must go!"

5 Use Your Gifts

Objectives
The children will:
- hear Romans 12:6-11.
- learn how Paul encouraged Christians in Rome to use the gifts God gave them.
- discover that they have been given gifts from God.
- explore what it means to use their gifts to do God's work.

Bible Story
Gifts from God
(Romans 12:6-11)

Bible Verse
You surround me—front and back.
    You put your hand on me. (Psalm 139:5)

Focus for the Teacher

Gifts from God
In a letter the apostle Paul wrote to Christians in Rome explaining his beliefs, he discusses spiritual gifts (Romans 12:9-11). Paul also discusses spiritual gifts in letters to the churches at Corinth (1 Corinthians 12) and Ephesus (Ephesians 4:11). The spiritual gifts Paul lists in these three letters are similar but not identical. It is likely that Paul meant none of these lists to be viewed as a complete inventory of possible spiritual gifts, but rather to serve as examples. God has blessed each one of us with unique abilities and gifts. All these gifts, whether or not they are mentioned in Paul's list, are important.

> God gave you gifts to use.

God Is All Around Us
The first four verses of Psalm 139 have thoroughly explored the idea that God knows us. God knows our actions, understands our plans, and is aware of the words we speak. The fifth verse of the psalm is a reassurance of God's presence. God knows us because God is with us. We are surrounded by God's presence and love.

Use Your Gifts
Whatever spiritual gifts we have been blessed with, Paul's instructions regarding these gifts are simple—use them! If your gift is serving, serve. If your gift is teaching, teach. (Thank you for using your gift of teaching!) If your gift is playing the trumpet, play. If your gift is drawing, draw. You get the idea. As you discuss spiritual gifts with the children this week, help them understand that all gifts can be used to do God's work. It is also appropriate to remind children that as we grow, we continue to discover and develop our gifts. God will continue to work in us and through us our entire lives. The work of God's spirit is not stagnant. We may receive new gifts as we grow older and gain life experience.

Explore Interest Groups

Be sure that adult leaders are waiting when the first child arrives. Greet and welcome the children. Get the children involved in an activity that interests them and introduces the theme for the day's activities.

Similar and Different

- **Say:** God made each of us unique. We can't all do the same things, and we aren't all interested in the same things. Imagine what a dull world it would be if we were all alike!

- Have each child find a partner.

- **Say:** Talk with your partner and discover one thing you both like to do. For example, perhaps you both like to dance, or maybe you are both good at helping people. Then discover something that is different—something one of you can do or likes to do that the other person can't do or doesn't like to do. For example, maybe one of you likes to cook and the other person doesn't, or perhaps one of you plays the trumpet and the other person plays the piano.

- Allow the children time to decide on similarities and differences.

- Have each pair of children combine with another pair to make groups of four.

- **Say:** Now in your groups of four, I would like you to do the same thing you did with your partner. Find one thing that all four of you like to do and one thing that is different about all four of you.

- Allow the children time to do the activity.

- Have each group of four combine with another group of four to make groups of eight.

- **Say:** In your group of eight, find one thing that all of you have in common and one thing that is different.

- Allow the children time to complete the task.

- If time permits have each child find a new partner and begin the activity again.

- **Ask:** Were you able to find similarities and differences regardless of how many people were in your group? Was it easier or more difficult the larger the group became?

- **Say:** Each one of us has different abilities and interests. One thing we all share is that God loves each and every one of us.

Prepare

✓ Provide paper, crayons, colored pencils, and markers.

✓ **Option:** Young children may draw pictures instead of writing words.

Words About Me

- Give each child a piece of paper.

- Have the children write their names in the middle of the paper using their favorite colors.

- **Ask:** If I asked you to describe yourself, what words would you use? What words would make people think about you? What words describe your interests?

- Allow children an opportunity to respond.

- Encourage the children to fill their paper with words that describe them.

- Invite children to share their artwork with each other.

Prepare

✓ Provide a mirror, paper, and crayons.

Self-Portraits Inside and Out

- Give each child a piece of paper and have the children fold it in half, bringing the short sides together.

- Invite the children to look in the mirror.

- **Ask:** What do you see?

- Encourage the children to draw a self-portrait on the outside of their paper.

- **Say:** When you look in the mirror, you can see the color of your eyes and the shape of your face. But the way you look isn't everything that makes you the person you are.

- **Ask:** What are some things about you that you can't see by looking in the mirror? For example, when you look in the mirror can you tell whether you like to read books?

- Encourage the children to write or draw on the inside of their paper some of the things about them that they can't see by looking in a mirror.

Large Group

Bring all the children together to experience the Bible story. Use a bell to alert the children to the large-group time.

Gifts from God

- **Say:** Our Bible story today is part of a letter that the apostle Paul wrote. Paul helped start many of the early churches. He also wrote letters to the churches to encourage them when he wasn't there.

- With the help of your recruited readers, read the Bible story in the "Gifts from God" handout.

- Thank your readers for using their gifts to help you tell the Bible story.

- **Ask:** How would you describe a gift from God? (Something God has given you—it might be a character trait, or knowledge, or ability) What are some of the gifts that Paul describes? (Telling people about God, serving, leading, teaching, encouraging, giving) Do you think there are other gifts from God that Paul has not talked about? (Yes)

- **Say:** Everything we have and everything we are is a gift from God. Just as there are many of us, there are many different gifts from God.

- **Ask:** No matter what gifts you have received from God, what does Paul say you should do with those gifts? (Use them.)

God Is All Around You

- **Say:** We have talked about God's promise to always be with us. God is all around us.

- Invite the children to read the Bible verse with you.

- **Say:** Now let's put some actions to our Bible verse.

- Have the children stand up.

- Teach the children the following actions:

  - o You surround me (Turn slowly in a circle.)
  - o front (Touch the front of your shoulders.)
  - o and back. (Touch the back of your shoulders.)
  - o You put your hand on me. (Give yourself a hug.)

Prepare

✓ Photocopy the "Gifts from God" handout at the end of this lesson for each child to take home.

✓ Recruit ten confident readers to help you tell the story.

✓ Give each reader a copy of the "Gifts from God" handout. Assign each reader one of the sentences following the introductory paragraph.

Prepare

✓ Write the Bible verses for the last four weeks and this week on a marker board or a piece of mural paper and place it where it can be easily seen. (LORD, you have examined me. You know me. You know when I sit down and when I stand up. Even from far away, you comprehend my plans. You study my traveling and resting. You are thoroughly familiar with all my ways. There isn't a word on my tongue, LORD, that you don't already know completely. You surround me—front and back. You put your hand on me. —Psalm 139:1-5)

✓ Cover verses 1-4 with a piece of paper so that only the verse for this week is visible.

✓ Review the actions for the previous verses.

- Encourage the children to say the Bible verse with you while doing the actions.

- Uncover the previous verses.

- **Say:** Now let's add this week's verse to our previous verses.

- Review the actions for the verses and then encourage the children to say all the verses with you while doing the actions.

Prepare

✓ Write each of the following words on a separate piece of paper: "talking," "serving," "encouragement," "giving," "leading."

You Can Use That Gift for God

- **Say:** Paul tells us that we need to use whatever gifts we are given. God can use our gifts and abilities and interests to do God's work. Let's think about the gifts Paul mentioned in his letter and how those gifts might be used to do God's work.

- One at a time, show the children the words you have written.

- **Ask:** If someone has this gift, what are some ways they could use that gift to do God's work?

- Allow the children an opportunity to answer. There are endless possibilities for each gift. Encourage the children to do some creative brainstorming.

- **Say:** Not only are there many different gifts, but there are also different ways to use each gift to do God's work.

- Dismiss children to their small groups.

Small Groups

Divide the children into small groups. You may organize the groups around age levels or around readers and nonreaders. Keep the groups small, with a maximum of ten children in each group. You may need to have more than one group of each age level.

Younger Children (Ages 5–7) and Older Children (Ages 8–11)

Note: This week all children will do the same activity in their small groups. It is still recommended that you divide children in age-specific groups so that discussion in the group can be age-appropriate.

- **Say:** We have been talking about gifts from God. Now each one of you will take some time to think about gifts that God has given you. One way to identify your gifts is to think about what you are able to do and what you like to do.

- Give each child a copy of the "My Gifts" handout and a pencil.

- Look at each section and allow each child an opportunity to write down his or her knowledge, abilities, and interests.

- If some children are having difficulty identifying their gifts, tell them something you notice that they know about, can do, or are interested in.

- **Say:** Take a look at all the things you have written on your paper. If you did the "Words About Me" activity earlier, also look at those words. Seeing all these words, how might you use your gifts to do God's work?

- Encourage each child to fill out the bottom section of the "My Gifts" handout.

- If a child is having difficulty coming up with ideas, invite him or her to share some of their information with the group and encourage the group to brainstorm about possible ways for that child to use his or her gifts.

- **Say:** Don't worry if you are not sure about how God wants you to use your gifts. As you grow older you will discover other gifts you have and find new ways to use them for God.

- **Pray:** God, everything we have is a gift from you. We thank you for the many gifts you have given us. Help us understand how you want us to use our gifts to do your work. Amen.

Prepare

✓ Photocopy the "My Gifts" handout at the end of this lesson for each child.

✓ Provide pencils.

✓ Ask children who completed the "Words About Me" activity to bring their papers to refer to.

Gifts from God

Based on Romans 12:6-11

The apostle Paul wrote lots of letters to churches encouraging them to keep up the good work. Paul wrote a letter to Christians who had started a church in Rome. Here are some of the things he told them.

We have all been given different gifts from God.

If your gift is the ability to tell people about God, then tell.

If your gift is serving, then serve.

If your gift is teaching, then teach.

If your gift is encouragement, then encourage.

If you are a giving person, then give.

If you are a leader, then lead.

Show love and hold onto what is good.

Honor each other's gifts.

Be enthusiastic—feel the excitement of the Spirit as you serve God!

My Gifts

Knowledge

Here are some things I know a lot about:

Abilities

Here are some things I can do and some things I am good at doing:

Interests

Here are some subjects I am interested in and some things I really enjoy:

I would like to use my gifts to do God's work. Here are some ideas about ways I might do that:

6 Keep Loving God

Objectives
The children will:
- hear Deuteronomy 6:4-9.
- learn about the Shema.
- discover that loving God involves your heart, your being, and your strength.
- explore what it means to keep loving God.

Bible Story
The Shema
(Deuteronomy 6:4-9)

Bible Verse
That kind of knowledge is too much for me;
    it's so high above me that I can't fathom it.
    (Psalm 139:6)

Focus for the Teacher

The Shema

"Love the LORD your God with all your heart, all your being, and all your strength."
(Deuteronomy 6:5)

People who speak Hebrew know this verse as part of the Shema. God instructed the Israelites to keep these words ever on their minds, teach them to their children, talk about them at home and away from home, and write them on their doorframes. These words are important! When asked for the greatest commandment, Jesus quoted these words (Matthew 22:36-40). Jesus went on to add a second commandment, "You must love your neighbor as yourself" (v. 39). Jesus explained that all the law and the prophets depend on these two commands.

> Stay close to God and learn what God wants you to do.

God's Knowledge Is Incomprehensible

With today's Bible verse we have learned the first six verses of Psalm 139. While the first five verses explored how completely God knows us, verse six is a response to being known by God. And the response is: that kind of knowledge is incomprehensible. God is God, and humans cannot fully understand the extent to which God knows us.

Keep Loving God
During this study we have discussed God's promise of continually being with us, God's plans for us, and God's ways of speaking to us; we have learned that we should stop making excuses and use our gifts to do God's work. The command to love God with our whole being links all these ideas together. When we stay in love with God, we are aware of God's presence in our lives, allowing us to be aware of God speaking to us. When we love God, we yearn to use our gifts to do God's work, which is us living out God's plans for our lives.

Explore Interest Groups

Be sure that adult leaders are waiting when the first child arrives. Greet and welcome the children. Get the children involved in an activity that interests them and introduces the theme for the day's activities.

Love God Door Hanger

- Give each child a door hanger.

- Have each child cut small pieces of construction paper and glue them onto his or her door hanger, overlapping the pieces slightly.

- Encourage each child to cover her or his entire door hanger, mosaic-style.

- Have the children write "Love God" on their door hangers.

- Invite the children to add other decorations to their door hangers as desired.

- **Say:** When you take your door hanger home, hang it where you will see it often. It will be a reminder to love God.

Prepare

✓ Cut the cardstock in half lengthwise. The finished door hanger will be 4¼ inches by 11 inches.

✓ Cut out a circle toward the top of each doorknob hanger. Make sure the circle is large enough to slip easily over a doorknob (approximately 2½ inches in diameter).

✓ Provide markers, construction paper, scissors, and glue sticks.

Musical Heart

- Have the children hold hands with one another and stand in a circle.

- **Ask:** What shape are we in now? (A circle)

- Choose two children on opposite sides of the circle.

- While the other children are still holding hands, have one of these two children walk about halfway to the center of the circle while the other child backs up an equal amount.

- **Ask:** What shape are we in now? (A heart)

- **Say:** Pay attention to where you are standing right now. We are going to go back to our circle shape and drop hands. I am going to play music while you begin walking around in a circle. When I stop the music, I want you to form our heart shape again.

- Give the children a moment to think about where they are standing and who is standing next to them.

Prepare

✓ Provide CD of Christian music and a CD player.

✓ Set up the CD player to play the music you have selected.

- Have the children return to a circle and drop hands.

- Tell the children which direction they are to walk.

- Begin playing music, and have the children begin walking.

- At a random time, stop the music.

- Encourage the children to form a heart shape.

- Repeat the activity a couple of times and see if it becomes easier for the children to re-form the heart.

- For an added challenge, have the children walk randomly around the room rather than around in a circle before re-forming the heart.

- **Say:** A heart is a symbol of love. Today we will talk about loving God.

Spell It Out

- **Say:** Today we are talking about loving God. You are going to spell out the words "Love God" with your bodies.

- Have the children work together to decide how to form each letter.

- Have the children lie on the floor and shape their bodies to form "Love God."

- Take a picture of the children forming each letter.

- Print out the pictures.

- Have the children glue the pictures in the correct order on the poster board.

- Invite the children to decorate the poster.

- Hang the poster where many people will see it.

Prepare

✓ Provide poster board, scissors, glue, a digital camera, and a method to print the photos.

✓ **Note:** If you do not have a digital camera or a way to print the photos, you can still do this activity and have the children form the letters.

✓ **Tip:** If you have a small class, form one letter at a time.

Large Group

Bring all the children together to experience the Bible story. Use a bell to alert the children to the large-group time.

The Shema

- **Say:** Moses is in our story today.

- **Ask:** What stories have we heard about Moses already? (Moses and the burning bush, Moses making excuses)

- Read the Bible story from "The Shema" handout.

- **Ask:** What do you think it means to love God with all your heart, being, and strength?

- Allow children time to share their ideas.

- **Say:** Jesus knew the importance of these words. When someone asked Jesus what the greatest commandment was, he quoted the Shema. "Love the Lord your God with all your heart, all your being, and all your strength." Jesus went on to say that the second greatest commandment is that we should love our neighbors as we love ourselves.

God Is Awesome

- **Say:** We have talked about how thoroughly God knows us. God knows us so completely that we really can't understand it. God is awesome and amazing!

- Invite the children to read the Bible verse with you.

- **Say:** Now let's put some actions to our Bible verse.

- Have the children stand up.

- Teach the children the following actions:

  o That kind of knowledge (Point to your forehead.)
  o is too much for me; (Begin with the palms of your hands together and then spread your hands as far apart as they will go.)
  o it's so high above me (Stand on tiptoes and reach as high as you can.)
  o that I can't fathom it. (Shrug and look puzzled.)

Prepare

✓ Photocopy "The Shema" handout at the end of this lesson for each child to take home.

Prepare

✓ Write the Bible verses for the last five weeks and this week on a marker board or a piece of mural paper and place it where it can be easily seen. (LORD, you have examined me. You know me. You know when I sit down and when I stand up. Even from far away, you comprehend my plans. You study my traveling and resting. You are thoroughly familiar with all my ways. There isn't a word on my tongue, LORD, that you don't already know completely. You surround me—front and back. You put your hand on me. That kind of knowledge is too much for me; it's so high above me that I can't fathom it. —Psalm 139:1-6)

✓ Cover verses one through five with a piece of paper so that only the verse for this week is visible.

✓ Review the actions for the previous verses.

- Encourage the children to say the Bible verse with you while doing the actions.

- Uncover the previous verses.

- **Say:** Now let's add this week's verse to our previous verses.

- Review the actions for the verses and then encourage the children to say all of the verses with you while doing the actions.

Loving God

- **Say:** It is one thing to say the words of the Shema, but we need to take the next step and put those words into action. Loving God with all our heart, all our being, and all our strength means that we are faithful to God, we love God more than anything, and we will serve God in every way we can.

- **Ask:** If these things are true, how will we act? What kind of things will we do? How will people be able to tell that we love God?

- Allow children an opportunity to share their ideas.

- **Say:** I have some questions for you. I hope that your answer will be an enthusiastic "Yes!"

- Ask the children the following questions and encourage them to respond, "Yes!"

  o Do you love God?
  o Do you love God with all your heart?
  o Do you love God with all your being?
  o Do you love God with all your strength?

- Dismiss children to their small groups.

Small Groups

Divide the children into small groups. You may organize the groups around age levels or around readers and nonreaders. Keep the groups small, with a maximum of ten children in each group. You may need to have more than one group of each age level.

Younger Children (Ages 5–7)

- Give each child a copy of the "Putting It All Together" handout.

- Have each child choose six different colors of crayons.

- **Say:** As we go over this worksheet together, follow the directions I give you.

- Read the following to the children, encouraging them to follow your instructions.

    o Choose one of your crayons and circle the words, "Love God." Of all the things we've talked about the last six weeks, loving God is the most important because loving God makes everything else we've talked about possible.
    o Choose a different color. Find the words, "God is with us," and circle them. Draw a line from these words to the words, "Love God." When we love God with our whole being we can feel God's presence.
    o Choose a different color. Find the words, "God has a plan in mind for us," and circle them. Draw a line from these words to the words, "Love God." When we love God and are in relationship with God, we want to keep trying to discover what God wants us to do.
    o Choose a different color. Find the words, "God sends us messages," and circle them. Draw a line from these words to the words, "Love God." When we love God we are paying attention to God. It is important to pay attention to messages God sends to us.
    o Choose a different color. Find the words, "God wants no excuses," and circle them. Draw a line from these words to the words, "Love God." When we love God, we trust God to give us the things we need to do God's work.
    o Choose a different color. Find the words, "God gives us gifts," and circle them. Draw a line from these words to the words, "Love God." When we love God, we want to use the gifts God gives us to do God's work. We want to share God's love with everyone we meet everywhere we go.

- **Ask:** How do we stay in love with God? What are some things we can do to be close to God?

Prepare

✓ Photocopy the "Putting It All Together" handout at the end of this lesson for each child.

✓ Provide crayons.

- Allow children an opportunity to share their ideas. There are many possible answers such as prayer, worship, attending Sunday school, reading the Bible, and so forth.

- **Say:** As you grow, you will discover more and more about your gifts and God's plans for you. Keep loving God, and God will guide you.

- **Pray:** God, we love you with all our heart, all our being, and all our strength! Guide us in your ways, and help us to live as you want us to live. Amen.

Prepare

✓ Photocopy the "Putting It All Together" handout at the end of this lesson for each child.

✓ Provide pencils.

Older Children (Ages 8–11)

- Give each child a copy of the "Putting It All Together" handout and a pencil.

- **Say:** We are going to look over this worksheet together and talk about the things we've been discussing the last six weeks.

- Lead the children through the following instructions and questions, allowing discussion after each question. Affirm the children's ideas and remember that there are multiple correct answers.

  o Circle the words, "Love God." Of all the things we've talked about the last six weeks, loving God is the most important because loving God makes everything else we've talked about possible.
  o Find the words, "God is with us," and circle them. Draw a line from these words to the words, "Love God."
  o **Ask:** What is the connection between loving God and knowing God is with us? (When we love God with our whole being we can feel God's presence.)
  o Find the words, "God has a plan in mind for us," and circle them. Draw a line from these words to the words, "Love God."
  o **Ask:** How does loving God help us discover God's plan? (When we love God and are in relationship with God, we want to keep trying to discover what God wants us to do.)
  o Find the words, "God sends us messages," and circle them. Draw a line from these words to the words, "Love God."
  o **Ask:** What is the relationship between loving God and receiving messages from God? (When we love God we are paying attention to God. It is important to pay attention to messages God sends us.)
  o Find the words, "God wants no excuses," and circle them. Draw a line from these words to the words, "Love God."

- o **Ask:** How does loving God make it easier to not make excuses about doing God's work? (When we love God, we trust God to give us the things we need to do God's work.)
- o Find the words, "God gives us gifts," and circle them. Draw a line from these words to the words, "Love God."
- o **Ask:** If we stay in love with God, what do we want to do with our gifts? (When we love God, we want to use the gifts God gives us to do God's work. We want to share God's love with everyone we meet everywhere we go.)

- **Ask:** How do we stay in love with God? What are the things we can do to be in relationship with God?

- Allow children an opportunity to share their ideas. There are many possible answers such as prayer, worship, attending Sunday school, reading the Bible, and so forth.

- **Say:** As you grow, you will discover more and more about your gifts and God's plans for you. Keep loving God and God will guide you.

- **Pray:** God, we love you with all our hearts, all our being, and all our strength! Guide us in your ways and help us to live as you want us to live. Amen.

The Shema

Based on Deuteronomy 6:4-9

Moses first heard God speaking from a burning bush. After Moses followed God's plan for him to help free the Israelites from slavery, God spoke to Moses many times. God gave Moses rules for the Israelites to follow so they would know how God wanted them to live.

Here is an important message that Moses relayed to God's people.

"Love the Lord your God with all your heart, all your being, and all your strength."

These words are sometimes called the Shema. Moses told the Israelites that these words were so important that they should always have them in mind. He said they should teach these words to their children. He told them to talk about these words when they were at home and when they were away from home. Moses told them they should write these words on their doorframes so they would see them every time they went through the door.

"Love the Lord your God with all your heart, all your being, and all your strength."

These were important words for the Israelites, and they are important words for us.

Putting It All Together

God is with us. God has a plan in mind for us. God sends us messages. God wants no excuses. God gives us gifts.

Love God

Made in the USA
Columbia, SC
04 March 2019